THE FARM

FARM MACHINERY

Ann Larkin Hansen
ABDO & Daughters

Published by Abdo & Daughters, 4940 Viking Drive, Suite 622, Edina, Minnesota 55435.

Copyright © 1996 by Abdo Consulting Group, Inc., Pentagon Tower, P.O. Box 36036, Minneapolis, Minnesota 55435 USA. International copyrights reserved in all countries. No part of this book may be reproduced in any form without written permission from the publisher.

Printed in the United States.

Cover Photo credits: Peter Arnold, Inc.
Interior Photo credits: Peter Arnold, Inc.

Edited by Bob Italia

Library of Congress Cataloging-in-Publication Data

Hansen, Ann Larkin.
    Farm Machinery / Ann Larkin Hansen
        p. cm. -- (The Farm)
    Includes index.
    Summary: Introduces various kinds of agricultural machinery, describes some of their major parts, and explains how these machines are used on the farm.
    ISBN 1-56239-622-6
    1. Agricultural Machinery--Juvenile literature. [1. Agricultural Machinery 2. Machinery.]
    I. Title. II. Series: Hansen, Ann Larkin. Farm.
    S675.25.H35 1996   96-11380
    631.3--dc20   CIP
                                                                                  AC

About the author

Ann Larkin Hansen has a degree in history from the University of St. Thomas in St. Paul, Minnesota. She currently lives with her husband and three boys on a farm in northern Wisconsin, where they raise beef cattle, chickens, and assorted other animals.

Contents

Tractors for Power

Tractors and farms go together like milk and cereal. Farmers need tractor power to pull the **implements** that plant and **harvest** crops. Between 1920 and 1950, tractors replaced horses on nearly all American farms.

Today's farms have two, three, or more tractors to do all the work. Because of tractors, farms are bigger than ever, and fewer workers are needed to run them.

The biggest tractors are built for the huge fields of the **western plains**. These monster machines are taller than a small house, and may turn 150 **horsepower** or more. You need a ladder to climb aboard, and there seem to be as many controls as an airplane!

Farmers need tractor power to pull their implements.

Parts of a Tractor

Every **tractor** has a **hitch** between the rear tires so **implements** can be attached. Many also have a **bucket** or scoop on the front. All but the oldest tractors have a **power takeoff** (PTO) for running different machines. This PTO is a short, rapidly-turning shaft that plugs into implements.

Most tractors also have **hydraulic** systems, an easy way to raise, lower, and turn implements. The back tires of a tractor are huge and usually filled not with air, but with a type of **antifreeze**. This gives them plenty of weight for good traction.

Opposite page:
The back tires of a tractor are huge, allowing for good traction.

The Dirt Busters

The first **implement** a farmer **hitches** to the **tractor** in the spring is the **plow**. The plow **bottoms** cut and turn the soil. Last year's weeds and plants are buried. Dirt is turned up for planting.

The **moldboard plow** has been used for hundreds of years. Today's farmers also use **chisel** plows and other new types. No matter what style, plows make it possible to grow a large amount of crops.

Opposite page: In some parts of the world, oxen are used for plowing.

Smoothers and Planters

A **plowed** field is full of big **clods** of upended dirt. Seeds don't sprout evenly in a lumpy field. With a **disc** or **harrow** behind the **tractor**, the farmer breaks up these clods and smooths the dirt.

Corn planters and **grain drills** are brought out next. Fifty-pound (23-kg) sacks of seed are dumped into the bins on the planters. As the tractor moves forward, metal discs on the planter open **furrows**, seed is dropped through tubes, and chains or discs push dirt over each seed.

Opposite page:
A farmer plowing a field.

Haymaking

When the alfalfa and clover begin to bloom, it is time to cut hay. **Mowers** or **haybines** 7 to 15 feet (2 to 4.5 m) wide leave the cut hay drying in long rows.

After a day or two of sun, the hay is raked into **windrows** with a hayrake. After a little more drying, the farmer **hitches** a **baler** and haywagon behind the **tractor**. The baler picks up the loose hay, and turns it into bales that shoot out the **kicker** and into the wagon. Some farmers use new types of balers to roll the hay into huge, round bales.

Opposite page:
The tractor pulls the
baler, which shoots the
baled hay onto a wagon.

Silage

In many parts of the country, farmers make **silage** instead of hay. Alfalfa, corn, or other green crops are cut and left to dry for only a day or two. Then they are chopped into small pieces with a **forage chopper** and blown into a **chopper box**, which looks like a covered hay wagon.

The box is hauled to the **silo**, and hooked to the **blower**. This blows the silage up a long tube into the silo. The farmer uses a **silo unloader** to push the silage down a chute when needed.

Grain silos in Kansas.

Harvest Time

Most corn and wheat is picked by **combines**. These huge machines pick the grain, strip off the **husks** or hulls, and spit out the leaves and stem. They are called combines because they combine the things that used to be done by separate **mowers** and **threshers**.

Potatoes, tomatoes, apples, rice and other crops are picked by specially made machines.

Opposite page:
Combining oats in Iowa.

Spreaders and Sprayers

Farmers know if they take crops from a field, they must give back **fertilizer** to get more crops next year. With a **manure spreader,** animal waste is scattered over the field. Other fertilizers come in bags and buckets, and are applied with special **sprayers** or spreaders.

If weeds or bugs threaten to kill or smother a crop, farmers can spray **chemicals** to kill them. But to keep **soils** healthy, fewer chemicals are needed.

Opposite page: A farmer with a manure spreader.

All-Terrain Vehicles

In the last ten years, a new farm machine, the **all-terrain vehicle (ATV)**, has appeared. It looks like a motorcycle with four wheels, and it isn't just for fun! Farmers use the ATV for all sorts of chores.

In the winter, ATVs haul hay for the animals, and firewood for the farmer. In the spring, ATVs can carry seed and lunches out to the field. In the summer and fall, fencing supplies are loaded up for repair crews.

Opposite page:
All-terrain vehicles
help move cattle.

Taking Care of Machinery

One of the most important jobs on a farm is fixing and maintaining all machinery. If the machines don't work, the farm won't work. When a breakdown happens, the farmer must have the tools and parts to fix it fast!

Greasing and oiling all moving parts is the best insurance against breakdowns. Farmers check bolts for tightness, tires for wear, and wires for **short-circuits**. The machines must be ready to go when they are needed.

Opposite page:
A farmer fixing a tractor.

All Kinds of Machines

There are many other kinds of farm **implements**. Farmers often make their own, or change what they have, to do a special job. There are machines that **hoe** weeds, shake apples off of trees, or dig ditches for drain tile. Everywhere there is a farm job, someone has made a machine to do it.

Tractors and implements are greasy and smelly. They take a lot of time to maintain and repair. But nothing beats the feeling when watching the **harvest** safely gathered with the help of smooth-running machinery!

Combining corn in Iowa.

Glossary

all-terrain vehicle (ATV) (all-tur-RAIN VEE-hick-ull)—a small, open vehicle with four to six large, soft tires.

antifreeze (ANN-tuh-freez)—a substance added to a liquid to lower its freezing point.

baler (BAY-ler)—a machine that takes loose hay and forms it into a round or square bundle.

blower—a machine that blows silage up a chute on the side and into the top of the silo.

bottoms—the part of the plow that cuts the dirt, consisting of the share, moldboard, landside, shin, and coverboard.

bucket—a metal scoop mounted on the front of many tractors.

chemical (KEM-ih-kull)—acids, bases, and gases used in chemistry.

chisel (CHIZZ-ull)—a type of plow blade with a narrow, cutting edge.

chopper box—a covered wagon used for transporting silage from the field.

clods—clumps or chunks of dirt.

combine (KAHM-bine)—a machine that cuts, threshes, and winnows grain in one continual operation. Most combines now are self-propelled; older ones were pulled by tractors.

corn planter—an implement that plants corn and other large seeds.

disc—an implement used to smooth soil.

fertilizer (FUR-tuh-lie-zer)—food for the soil, to make crops grow.

forage chopper—a machine that chops standing green plants into short pieces.

furrow—a groove made in the ground by a plow.

grain drill—an implement designed to plant small seeds such as oats. Many drills have grass-seeder attachments for very tiny seeds.

harrow—an implement that smooths the soil.

harvest—bringing the crops in from the fields. Harvest can also mean the crops themselves.

haybine—a machine that cuts hay and then crimps it with rollers to make it dry faster.

hitch—to attach an implement to the tractor; or, the way in which an implement is attached. Most common are the quick-hitch and the three-point hitch.

hoe—to loosen soil or cut small weeds.

horsepower—a unit for measuring the power of an engine.

husk—the dry outer covering of seeds or fruits.

hydraulics (hi-DRAWL-icks)—a system for lifting, turning, and powering various implements by means of liquid forced through hoses.

implement (IM-pluh-ment)—On a farm, an implement is a tool designed to be operated by hitching to a tractor.

kicker—a baler attachment that shoots the bales out the back end of the baler and into the haywagon.

manure spreader—an implement for spreading manure.

moldboard plow—a curved iron plate attached above a plowshare to lift and turn the soil.

mower—an implement that cuts hay.

plow—an implement that breaks up the soil to make ready for planting.

power takeoff (PTO)—a rotating shaft between the back tractor wheels. It powers many types of implements and is extremely dangerous.

short circuit (short SIR-kit)—when insulation wears off wires which touch each other. A short circuit may blow a fuse or cause a fire.

silage (SIE-laj)—any green plants chopped fine and stored in a silo for later feeding. Corn silage is most common.

silo—Tall, tubular cement or metal structures for storing silage.

silo unloader—a machine inside the silo for pushing out silage, usually in the top of the silo.

soil (SOY-ull)—part of the earth's surface that plants are grown in; dirt.

sprayer—an implement with tanks and spray equipment made for covering large areas.

thresher—no longer commonly seen, threshers beat grain free of the leaves and stalks. They have been replaced by combines, along with reapers, binders, and cleaners.

tractor—a machine designed specifically for the specialized power needs of farmers. They have gas or diesel engines, special tires, and various other special features.

western plains—a vast flat region in western North America extending for about 2,500 miles (4,023 km) from Alberta, Canada to Texas, consisting of flat treeless land.

windrow—a row of raked hay running the length of the field.

Index